W9-AAD-592

Hidden Pictures®
Two-Player Puzzles

HIGHLIGHTS PRESS
Honesdale, Pennsylvania

Two Can Play

This book is full of fun puzzles for friends or family to do together, but in lots of different ways. For some puzzles, you'll work together. For other puzzles, you'll race your opponent. Sometimes you'll sit side-by-side, and sometimes you'll sit across from each other.

Side-by-Side Puzzles

Seeing Double 4, 28, 52, 76, 100, 124
Take Two 6, 30, 54, 78, 102, 126
Color Teamwork 14, 38, 62, 86, 110, 134
Mirror, Mirror 16, 40, 64, 88, 112, 136
Words and Objects 22, 46, 70, 94, 118

These Games!

Sitting Opposite Puzzles*

Silly Fill-In Story. 8, 32, 56, 80, 104, 128
Twice as Nice. 12, 36, 60, 84, 108, 132
Guess and Seek. 18, 42, 66, 90, 114
Hide It! 24, 48, 72, 96, 120

*Some of these puzzles have a page in between them with directions. You should hold up this page while you play so you can't peek at what your partner is doing!

Seeing Double

Each object is hidden twice—once in each scene. Race your opponent to see who can find all 12 objects in his or her scene first!

flag

key

apple

pickle

shoe

cupcake

mitten

horseshoe

dog bone

lollipop

boot

pear

Art by Linda Davick

5

Take Two

Each of these scenes contains 12 hidden objects, which are listed on the right. But each object is hidden only once. Which object is in which scene? Work with a friend to find all the objects.

ax
crayon
glove
radish
tack

bottle
crescent moon
harmonica
sailboat
toothbrush

bowling ball
drinking straw
mallet
shoe
wedge of cheese

button
fish
peanut
slice of orange
yo-yo

cane
flashlight
pineapple
slice of pie

Art by Neil Numberman

Art by David Helton

Silly Fill-In Story

Hold up this page and start searching for the 12 objects hidden in the picture. When you find an object, tell your friend the name of that object.

Dog School

golf club

boot

sailboat

book

kite

sock

bow tie

leaf

fried egg

hockey stick

feather

pie

Silly Fill-In Story

Hold up this page. When your friend tells you the name of an object, write the name of that object in the first blank. Continue until all of the blanks are filled.

Dog School

"Sit!" "Stay!" " _Drake_ !" Sure, we dogs know all these basic
                    1

commands. But at Ms. Trixie's School for _good on lead_ Dogs, we learn
                                              2

new tricks every day. Today we learned that it is not all right to chew a

_____ or scratch a person's _____, but it is OK to shake
      3   4

paws with a _____. That news totally made my _____
                  5   6

wag. In class, I sit next to a pug named Charlie. He is very nice, but he can't

seem to tell his _____ from his _____! Ms. Trixie
                        7   8

has been working extra hard with him. Today, after he fetched the squeaky-

toy _____ from the back of the room, she gave him a peanut-
          9

butter-covered _____. I hope I earn one of those tomorrow! For
                      10

homework tonight, we each need to bark at a _____ once and sniff
                                                     11

a _____ twice. I think I can handle it!
       12

Twice as Nice

The hidden words your partner is finding are hidden objects, too. Can you find these 13 objects in the scene below?

fork

broccoli

carrot

domino

ruler

drinking straw

lollipop

worm

slice of pizza

horseshoe

banana

bird

book

Twice as Nice

The hidden objects your partner is finding are hidden words, too. Can you find these 13 words in the letters below?

L	D	R	I	B	K	H	Y	R	S	C	D	P	V	H	D
W	H	I	R	M	K	S	A	X	A	X	A	W	D	A	A
G	L	O	L	L	I	P	O	P	B	R	Y	F	E	M	I
D	R	I	N	K	I	N	G	S	T	R	A	W	R	S	A
A	L	I	L	R	I	U	H	I	Y	O	N	O	X	N	H
Z	K	X	Q	U	T	W	B	O	E	T	W	X	A	J	L
Y	D	D	B	L	B	I	Y	D	O	M	I	N	O	G	G
S	L	I	C	E	O	F	P	I	Z	Z	A	R	E	K	O
A	M	E	H	R	L	M	O	U	B	H	P	F	E	G	G
B	H	O	R	S	E	S	H	O	E	T	T	A	C	S	I
V	S	Y	N	B	W	Z	D	P	W	K	T	M	K	I	W
E	Q	I	N	B	K	A	A	P	M	Y	Y	O	L	G	W
H	F	O	R	K	U	M	G	B	W	J	O	H	I	T	X
J	B	R	O	C	C	O	L	I	G	B	W	I	K	J

Word List

BANANA
BIRD
BOOK
BROCCOLI
CARROT
DOMINO
DRINKING STRAW
FORK
HORSESHOE
LOLLIPOP
RULER
SLICE OF PIZZA
WORM

13

Color Teamwork

seal

pencil

bird

heart

crown

crescent moon

Don't let this game pull you apart! Work with your teammate to find all 12 objects in this scene. Then color it in together.

 mitten

carrot

banana

 domino

 doughnut

 book

Mirror, Mirror

Each of these scenes contains the same 14 hidden objects, which are listed on the right. But the scenes are flip-flopped. Race your opponent to see who can find all 14 objects in his or her scene first!

baseball
paintbrush
ring
toothbrush

envelope
paper clip
slice of lemon
umbrella

fishhook
peanut
teacup

golf tee
pencil
thermometer

Art by Daryll Collins

17

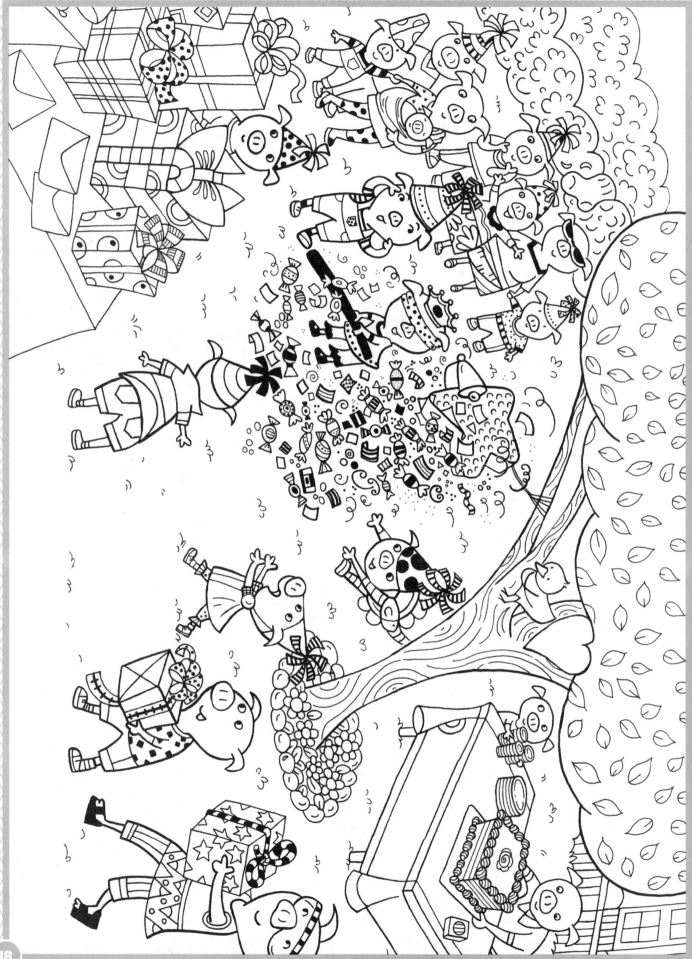

Guess and Seek

These are the 12 objects hidden in your friend's scene. Hold up this page and describe an object for your friend to find—without using its name. For example, you might describe a lollipop as a piece of candy on a stick.

Take turns with your friend describing and finding objects. While your friend is finding objects, you can color in your scene.

lollipop

paintbrush

light bulb

ball of yarn

heart

ring

horseshoe

cowboy hat

candle

fish

sock

toothbrush

Pig Piñata Party

Guess and Seek

These are the 12 objects hidden in your friend's scene. Hold up this page and describe an object for your friend to find—without using its name. For example, you might describe a sock as a glove for your foot.

Take turns with your friend describing and finding objects. While your friend is finding objects, you can color in your scene.

 candy cane

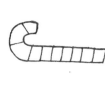 bell

heart

kite

fish

sock

 toothbrush

pencil

cheese

carrot

crescent moon

megaphone

Pig Pie Party

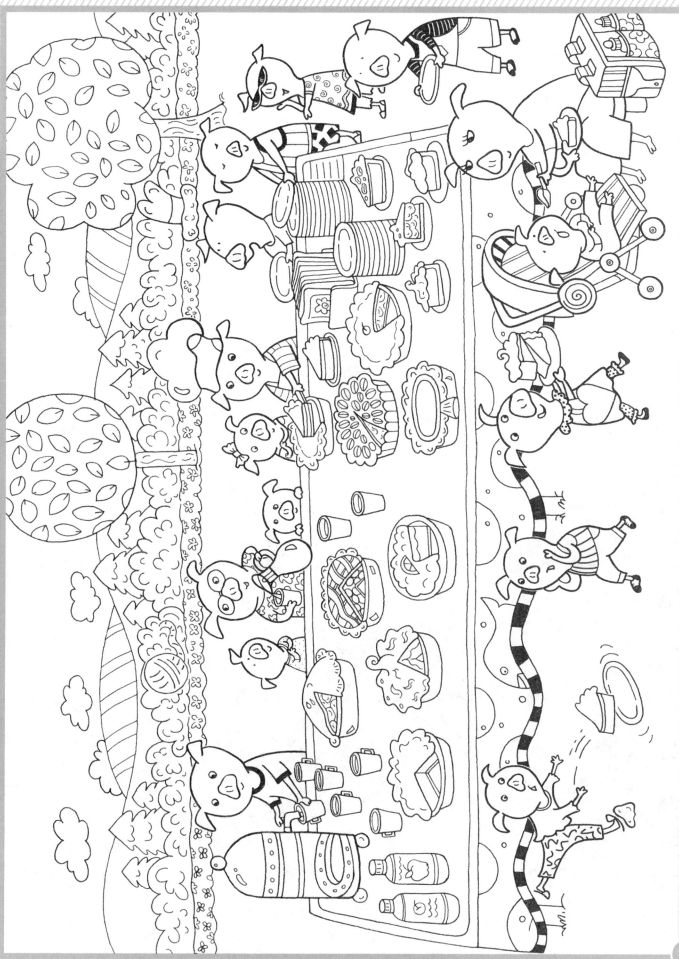

Words and Objects

There are 8 OBJECTS hidden on this page that match the 8 WORDS hidden on the next page. Work together to find them all.

There are 8 WORDS hidden on this page that match the 8 OBJECTS hidden on the previous page. Work together to find them all.

Art by Brian White

hide it!

Can you hide a banana like the one below in a drawing? Hold up this page and draw your own Hidden Pictures® scene. Here are some ideas.

When you're finished, turn the book around so your friend can solve your Hidden Pictures® puzzle!

Hide It!

Can you hide an ice-cream cone like the one below in a drawing? Hold up this page and draw your own Hidden Pictures® scene. Here are some ideas.

When you're finished, turn the book around so your friend can solve your Hidden Pictures® puzzle!

Seeing Double

Each object is hidden twice—once in each scene. Race your opponent to see who can find all 12 objects in his or her scene first!

parachute　skateboard　fan　camera　mouse　box

tack　star　rocket ship　butterfly　flower　ring

Art by Linda Davick

29

Take Two

Each of these scenes contains 12 hidden objects, which are listed on the right. But each object is hidden only once. Which object is in which scene? Work with a friend to find all the objects.

Art by Neil Numberman

The Hopping _____ Bakery offers the best carrot cake, _____
                        1   2

cookies, and sweet _____ bread that money can buy. The bakery has only
                             3

been open for a year, yet these hardworking bunnies have already won the hearts—

and stomachs—of everyone in _____ City. The talented owner first learned
                                       4

to bake by mixing up a _____ with a _____ and calling it
                                   5   6

Whipped _____ Delight. Today his specialty is creating the perfect four-layer
                    7

_____ to enjoy at weddings. Some people are surprised to learn that a little
         8

furry _____ can create such treats. But it's true. Once a customer tastes the
                  9

chocolate _____ or samples just a lick of a powdered _____,
                     10   11

they learn the truth about bunnies. They can bake better than any _____ out
                                                                              12

there. Stop by today!

Silly Fill-In Story

Hold up this page. When your friend tells you the name of an object, write the name of that object in the first blank. Continue until all of the blanks are filled.

Bunny Bakery

Silly Fill-In Story

Hold up this page and start searching for the 12 objects hidden in the picture.
When you find an object, tell your friend the name of that object.

Bunny Bakery

crown

bell

heart

hammer

purse

megaphone

cherry

pumpkin

candle

pencil

shoe

toothbrush

Art by Mike DeSantis

The hidden objects your partner is finding are hidden words, too. Can you find these 14 words in the letters below?

Word List

BANANA
BASEBALL
DOG BONE
FEATHER
FLAG
FORK
FUNNEL
GOLF CLUB
ICE-CREAM
CONE
SCISSORS
SHOE
SPOON
TEACUP
WORM

```
N W I A F H F L I U T E K K C
R O Q C L U E E N X B E F O R K
F R G E U N O A B K B A N A N A
J M P C O N O T N J C F Q W E
Z X Z R Z E G H T N S U P V S
O O S E P L P E Y V P P N S S H
N W B A T V D R M R S V K J O
Q U N M H M F V C M C P T S Y E
C Y B C G O L F C L U B T F N G
Y L S O N A P T R T U G W O A J
R T U N J S P O O N J B B L A R
B A S E B A L L D O L G F S B G
B F S C I S S O R S O T S X P I
E Y R L M P I D W L Q Q N L
```

worm

 feather

 shoe

 flag

 baseball

 dog bone

 banana

Twice as Nice

The hidden words your partner is finding are hidden objects, too. Can you find these 14 objects in the scene below?

 funnel

 teacup

 scissors

 ice-cream cone

 fork

 spoon

 golf club

Color Teamwork

 hummingbird   ladybug   banana   lollipop   butterfly   feather   kite

Trapeze school is a barrel of fun with a partner. Work with your teammate to find all 14 objects in this scene. Then color it in together.

arrow   airplane   leaf   fish   lightning bolt   fork   pineapple

Mirror, Mirror

Each of these scenes contains the same 17 hidden objects, which are listed on the right. But the scenes are flip-flopped. Race your opponent to see who can find all 17 objects in his or her scene first!

artist's brush

banana

candle

colored pencil

crown

envelope

flag

flashlight

ice-cream cone

light bulb

needle

paintbrush

ruler

slice of pie

star

toothbrush

wishbone

Art by Nuno Alexandre Vieira

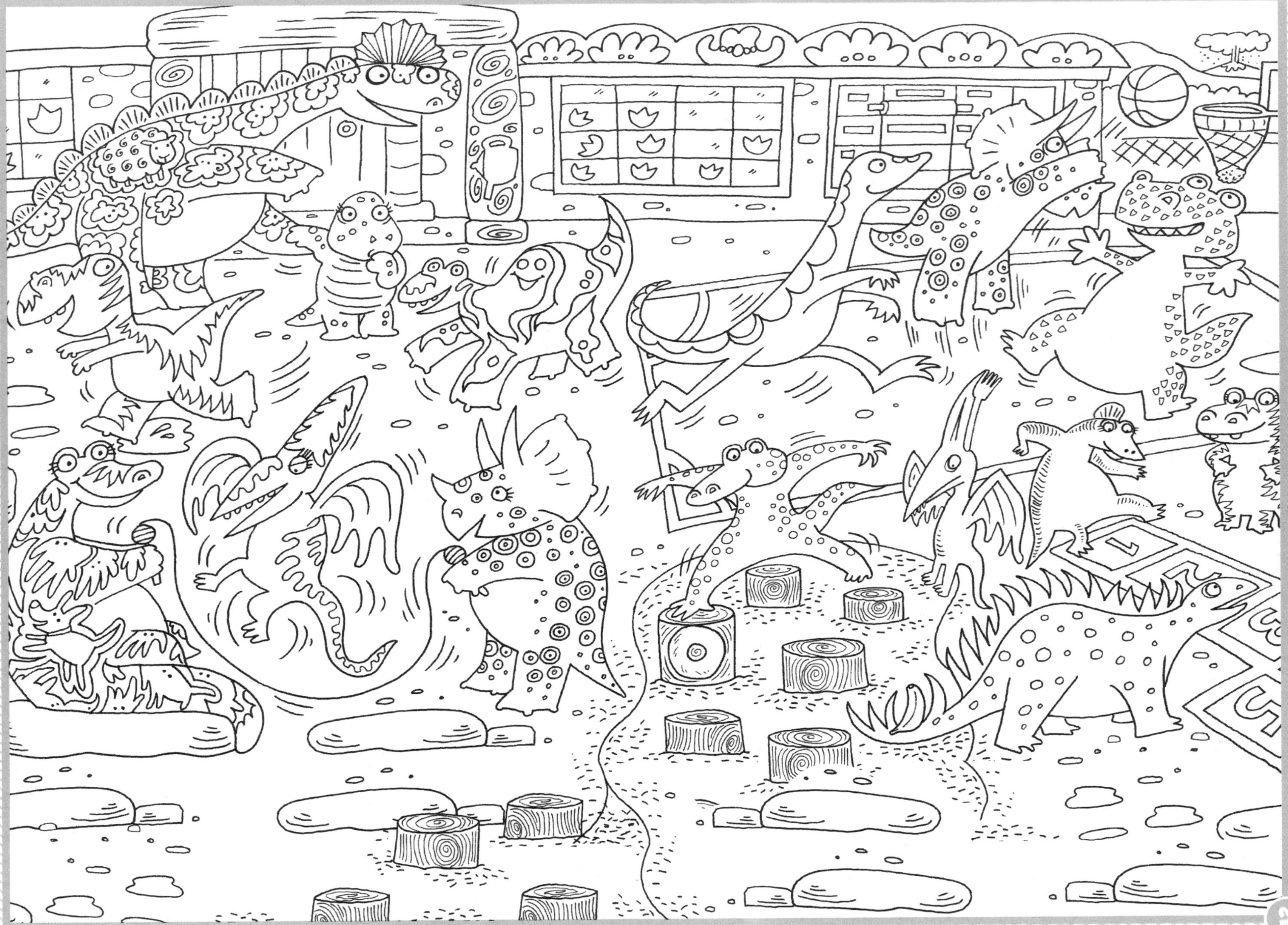

Art by Beccy Blake

Guess and Seek

These are the 12 objects hidden in your friend's scene. Hold up this page and describe an object for your friend to find—without using its name. For example, you might describe broccoli as a green vegetable that looks like a tree.

Take turns with your friend describing and finding objects. While your friend is finding objects, you can color in your scene.

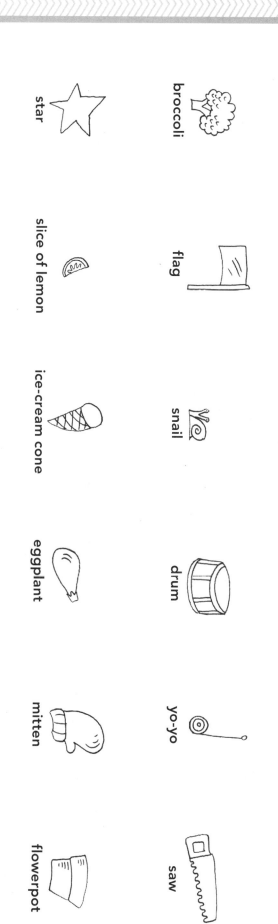

broccoli

star

flag

snail

slice of lemon

ice-cream cone

drum

yo-yo

eggplant

mitten

saw

flowerpot

Guess and Seek

These are the 12 objects hidden in your friend's scene. Hold up this page and describe an object for your friend to find—without using its name. For example, you might describe a banana as a yellow fruit.

Take turns with your friend describing and finding objects. While your friend is finding objects, you can color in your scene.

banana

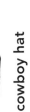

pine tree

wool hat

cowboy hat

crescent moon

bagel

ghost

rolling pin

dog

teapot

sheep

fork

Balloon Toss

Words and Objects

There are 8 WORDS hidden on this page that match the 8 OBJECTS hidden on the next page. Work together to find them all.

There are 8 OBJECTS hidden on this page that match the 8 WORDS hidden on the previous page. Work together to find them all.

Art by Iryna Bodnaruk

Hide It!

Can you hide a sock like the one below in a drawing? Hold up this page and draw your own Hidden Pictures® scene. Here are some ideas.

When you're finished, turn the book around so your friend can solve your Hidden Pictures® puzzle!

Hide It!

Can you hide a crayon like the one below in a drawing? Hold up this page and draw your own Hidden Pictures® scene. Here are some ideas.

When you're finished, turn the book around so your friend can solve your Hidden Pictures® puzzle!

Seeing Double

Each object is hidden twice—once in each scene. Race your opponent to see who can find all 12 objects in his or her scene first!

acorn

adhesive bandage

football

fried egg

worm

olive

cookie

hot dog

binoculars

boomerang

slice of lime

needle

Art by Amy Schimler-Safford

Take Two

Each of these scenes contains 12 hidden objects, which are listed on the right. But each object is hidden only once. Which object is in which scene? Work with a friend to find all the objects.

anchor
banana
bat (animal)
cane
canoe

cupcake
drinking straw
glove
hammer
harmonica

ice-cream cone
ladder
magnet
mushroom
open book

paintbrush
pencil
ruler
skateboard
slice of cake

sock
toaster
toothbrush
yo-yo

Art by Neil Numberman

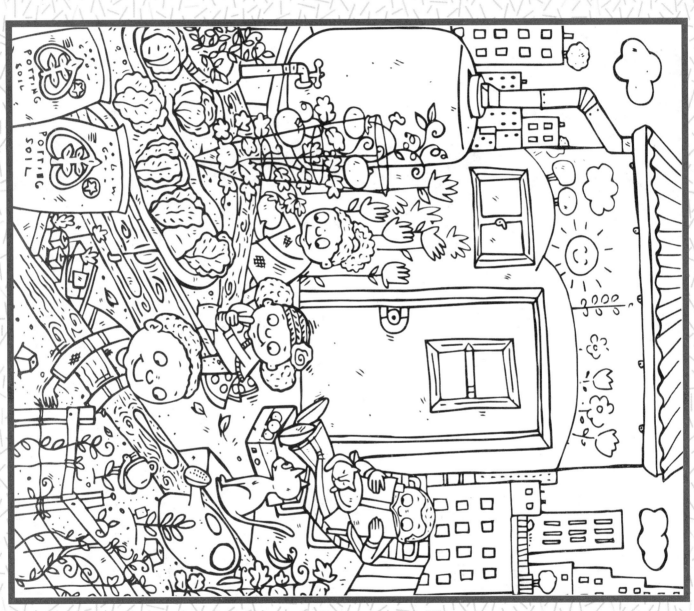

Silly Fill-In Story

Hold up this page and start searching for the 12 objects hidden in the picture. When you find an object, tell your friend the name of that object.

City Garden

 goblet

 teacup

 pizza

 boot

 ice-cream cone

 magnet

 spoon

 pennant

 golf club

 spatula

 toothbrush

pencil

Silly Fill-In Story

Hold up this page. When your friend tells you the name of an object, write the name of that object in the first blank. Continue until all of the blanks are filled.

City Garden

Last spring, Dad said he wanted to plant a garden on the _____ 1

on our apartment building. His exact words were, "I love dirt, I love my

_____ 2 , and I love to eat a fresh _____ with dinner, so let's

plant a _____ 4 !" Mom laughed and said that she didn't have time to 3

put her hands in a dirty _____ 5 . Dad had time, and he decided that his

_____ 6 did, too. At first we said, "No _____ 7 !" But Dad said

it would be good for us. It turns out he was right. Not only is gardening fun—I like

the feel of _____ 8 under may nails and the smell of _____ 9

on my clothes!—but it is also rewarding. Today, after caring for our garden for so

long, we picked our first green _____ 10 . It was delicious! For dinner,

we are going to mix some of the fresh _____ 11 with salt, pepper, and

_____ 12 to make the perfect feast.

Twice as Nice

The hidden words your partner is finding are hidden objects, too. Can you find these 14 objects in the scene below?

fan

baseball

cane

horseshoe

slice of lemon

wishbone

carrot

feather

lime

button

doughnut

butterfly

grapes

sock

Twice as Nice

The hidden objects your partner is finding are hidden words, too. Can you find these 14 words in the letters below?

H N A T Q N C A R R O T P Y Q C
O S Z P K F F B T J Y T P E W G
R W W S L I C E O F L E M O N D
S J W F E A T H E R I L Y V V W
E S I P D Y M N T L Q L N M W
S B S O O M A Z A V Y F O Q O L
H A H J U C V N C S R T Q M Y R
O S B S G N A N W E T B F Z C E
E E O L H F Y N T U T Q T N L
X B N K N A N T B C P S U C N L
C A E E U V U E F H X D S T M
C L H N T B Y G R A P E S N V F
Q L I A C P J W P I W D E Y S Y
H N S O C K K G W N T A L I M

Word List

BASEBALL

BUTTERFLY

BUTTON

CANE

CARROT

DOUGHNUT

FAN

FEATHER

GRAPES

HORSESHOE

LIME

SOCK

SLICE OF
LEMON

WISHBONE

Color Teamwork

cupcake

bat

light bulb

chicken drumstick

toothbrush

sock

mitten

Pass the ball to score a touchdown! Work with your teammate to find all 14 objects in this scene. Then color it in together.

Art by Mike Dammer

seashell   ruler   ice-cream cone   spoon   banana   mug   ladder

Mirror, Mirror

Each of these scenes contains the same 14 hidden objects, which are listed on the right. But the scenes are flip-flopped. Race your opponent to see who can find all 14 objects in his or her scene first!

bowling ball
crayon
drinking straw
drumstick

golf club
handbag
hat
horseshoe

ice-cream cone
lollipop
macaroni noodle

sailboat
tack
toothbrush

Art by Neil Numberman

Guess and Seek

These are the 12 objects hidden in your friend's scene. Hold up this page and describe an object for your friend to find—without using its name. For example, you might describe a kite as a diamond-shaped toy that can fly.

Take turns with your friend describing and finding objects. While your friend is finding objects, you can color in your scene.

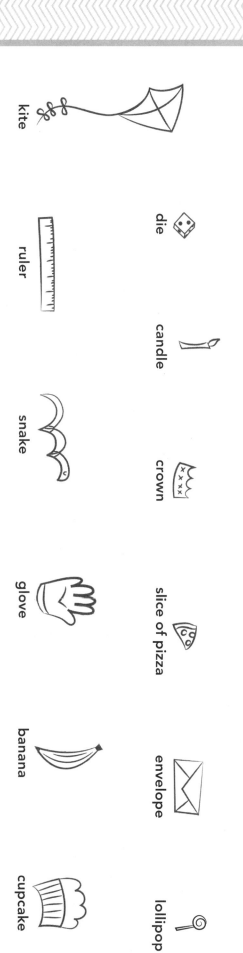

kite

die

ruler

candle

snake

crown

slice of pizza

glove

banana

envelope

lollipop

cupcake

Pretty Peacocks

Guess and Seek

These are the 12 objects hidden in your friend's scene. Hold up this page and describe an object for your friend to find—without using its name. For example, you might describe an apple as a fruit that's red.

Take turns with your friend describing and finding objects. While your friend is finding objects, you can color in your scene.

kite

fried egg

anchor

ice-cream cone

sailboat

apple

comb

baseball

heart

fish

leaf

banana

Flamingo Flamenco

Words and Objects

There are 8 OBJECTS hidden on this page that match the 8 WORDS hidden on the next page. Work together to find them all.

There are 8 WORDS hidden on this page that match the 8 OBJECTS hidden on the previous page. Work together to find them all.

Art by Howard McWilliam

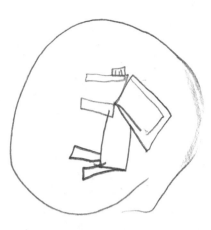

Hide It!

Can you hide a toothbrush like the one below in a drawing? Hold up this page and draw your own Hidden Pictures® scene. Here are some ideas.

When you're finished, turn the book around so your friend can solve your Hidden Pictures® puzzle!

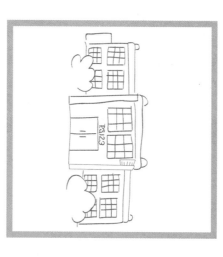

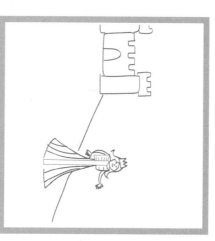

Hide It!

Can you hide a baseball bat like the one below in a drawing? Hold up this page and draw your own Hidden Pictures® scene. Here are some ideas.

When you're finished, turn the book around so your friend can solve your Hidden Pictures® puzzle!

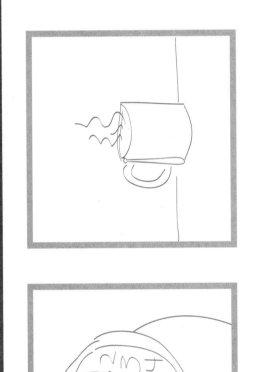

Seeing Double

Each object is hidden twice—once in each scene. Race your opponent to see who can find all 12 objects in his or her scene first!

briefcase · egg · book · envelope · canoe · slice of bread

clothespin · trowel · snail's shell · bucket · spoon · necktie

Art by Linda Davick

77

Take Two

Each of these scenes contains 12 hidden objects, which are listed on the right. But each object is hidden only once. Which object is in which scene? Work with a friend to find all the objects.

apple · carrot · hedgehog · pyramid · squash

artist's brush · crown · key · rubber duck · toothbrush

ax · envelope · light bulb · ruler · wedge of cheese

baseball bat · fork · lizard · saltshaker · wristwatch

bell · giraffe · pear · snake

Art by Iryna Bodnaruk

My name is Ozzie Ostrich, and I run the best bird tour company in the whole feathered world. Birds flock from the south, the north, and even the icy _____ to ride
1

in Ozzie's Balloons. My guests today included a young _____ from Spain,
2

her elderly _____, and a purple _____ who was visiting from
3   4

Australia. We soared high above the _____ and looked at the beautiful,
5

faraway _____. Then, one guest leaned too far out of the _____
6   7

and nearly fell overboard! He was a barnyard _____ who never
8

learned to fly, so he wouldn't have been able to fly to safety! Thinking fast, I thrust a

_____ in his direction. He grabbed on with his _____ and I
9   10

pulled him up into the balloon! He was so grateful he gave me a big _____.
11

I put my wing around him and we enjoyed the rest of the lovely _____
12

together. Just another day on the job.

Silly Fill-In Story

Hold up this page. When your friend tells you the name of an object, write the name of that object in the first blank. Continue until all of the blanks are filled.

Bird's-Eye View

Silly Fill-In Story

Hold up this page and start searching for the 12 objects hidden in the picture. When you find an object, tell your friend the name of that object.

Bird's-Eye View

crescent moon

spool of thread

 bananas

 magnet

computer monitor

pencil

sailboat

can opener

spoon

glove

 cane

 musical note

Twice as Nice

The hidden objects your partner is finding are hidden words, too. Can you find these 14 words in the letters below?

Word List

BANANA
BROOM
CARROT
CRAYON
CRESCENT
MOON
FISH
GOLF CLUB
KITE
LEAF
SALTSHAKER
SLICE OF PIE
SOCK
SPOON
TOOTH

F	S	U	U	W	N	M	D	U	D	T	X	Y	S	G	N
I	L	L	C	R	A	Y	O	N	M	O	N	L	X	A	X
I	F	O	D	J	R	G	T	I	U	O	R	B	Q	L	R
K	A	F	S	N	W	F	H	S	O	T	F	J	Z	U	Y
I	K	J	G	D	V	U	M	K	H	C	I	S	M	Y	
T	J	H	Q	M	L	U	T	C	V	I	R	G	W	E	H	O
E	B	R	O	O	M	N	O	N	I	R	S	S	P	I	
E	U	D	W	T	E	S	A	L	T	S	H	A	K	E	R
F	S	L	I	C	E	O	F	P	I	E	B	M	L	M	C
U	D	R	S	L	O	N	O	Q	E	F	A	F	E	A	
F	I	E	S	Y	W	E	U	H	J	N	F	A	N	R	
R	R	Q	B	S	P	O	O	N	M	L	A	Z	F	D	R
C	I	W	V	M	B	H	J	F	G	A	N	U	S	O	
T	Z	U	G	O	L	F	C	L	U	B	A	V	J	U	T

Twice as Nice

The hidden words your partner is finding are hidden objects, too. Can you find these 14 objects in the scene below?

 spoon

 slice of pie

 crayon

 kite

 tooth

 sock

 carrot

 crescent moon

 leaf

 banana

 fish

 saltshaker

 broom

 golf club

Art by Jackie Stafford

Color Teamwork

 kite sock slice of pizza snake saw teacup turtle

Stop monkeying around! Work with your teammate to find all 14 objects in this scene. Then color it in together.

trowel   safety pin   comb   whale   ax   sailboat   ladder

Art by Tamara Petrosino

Mirror, Mirror

Each of these scenes contains the same 15 hidden objects, which are listed on the right. But the scenes are flip-flopped. Race your opponent to see who can find all 15 objects in his or her scene first!

crown   fishhook   paper airplane   spoon

diamond   flashlight   pencil   toothbrush

domino   flyswatter   plunger   top hat

drinking straw   ladle   slice of orange

Art by Neil Numberman

Guess and Seek

These are the 12 objects hidden in your friend's scene. Hold up this page and describe an object for your friend to find—without using its name. For example, you might describe a ring as a piece of jewelry that goes on your finger.

Take turns with your friend describing and finding objects. While your friend is finding objects, you can color in your scene.

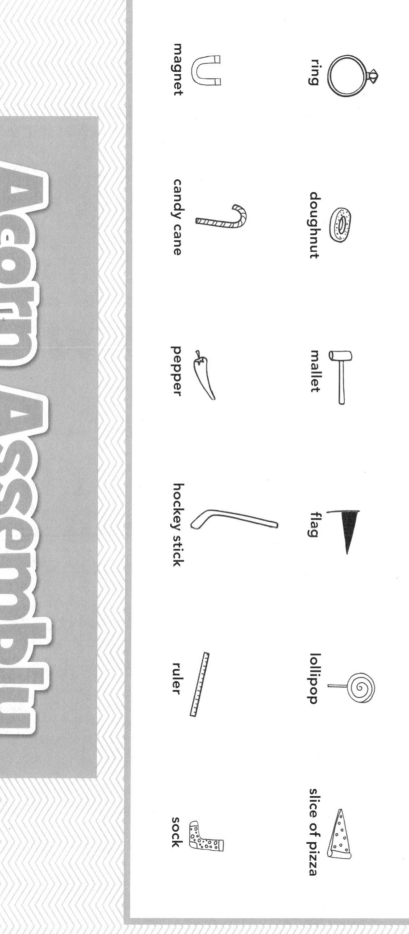

ring

doughnut

mallet

flag

lollipop

slice of pizza

magnet

candy cane

pepper

hockey stick

ruler

sock

Acorn Assembly

Guess and Seek

These are the 12 objects hidden in your friend's scene. Hold up this page and describe an object for your friend to find—without using its name. For example, you might describe a doughnut as a sugary treat with a hole in the middle.

Take turns with your friend describing and finding objects. While your friend is finding objects, you can color in your scene.

screwdriver

button

paintbrush

slice of watermelon

glove

doughnut

envelope

fish

fishhook

teddy bear

horseshoe

four-leaf clover

Honey Hive

Words and Objects

There are 8 WORDS hidden on this page that match the 8 OBJECTS hidden on the next page. Work together to find them all.

There are 8 OBJECTS hidden on this page that match the 8 WORDS hidden on the previous page. Work together to find them all.

Art by Brian White

hide it!

Can you hide a crescent moon like the one below in a drawing? Hold up this page and draw your own Hidden Pictures® scene. Here are some ideas.

When you're finished, turn the book around so your friend can solve your Hidden Pictures® puzzle!

Hide It!

Can you hide a heart like the one below in a drawing? Hold up this page and draw your own Hidden Pictures® scene. Here are some ideas.

When you're finished, turn the book around so your friend can solve your Hidden Pictures® puzzle!

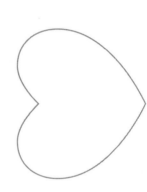

Seeing Double

Each object is hidden twice—once in each scene. Race your opponent to see who can find all 12 objects in his or her scene first!

flowerpot · knitted hat · mug · in-line skate · kite · football · sock · car · button · toothbrush · glove · hammer

Take Two

Each of these scenes contains 12 hidden objects, which are listed on the right. But each object is hidden only once. Which object is in which scene? Work with a friend to find all the objects.

banana
bird
canoe
chef's hat
desk bell

dolphin
envelope
feather
fishhook
flashlight

frying pan
funnel
hockey stick
ice-cream cone
ice skate

leaf
mug
pencil
plunger
saltshaker

scissors
screwdriver
shuttlecock
wedge of cheese

Silly Fill-In Story

Hold up this page and start searching for the 12 objects hidden in the picture. When you find an object, tell your friend the name of that object.

Dreamy Art

tennis racket

carrot

magnifying glass

feather

bread

boot

ladder

pear

envelope

toothbrush

fried egg

dog bone

Silly Fill-In Story

Hold up this page. When your friend tells you the name of an object, write the name of that object in the first blank. Continue until all of the blanks are filled.

Dreamy Art

Today's art class was highly unusual. First, our teacher gave us each a piece of

_____ 1 _____ and told us to draw on it with a fine-tipped

_____ 2 _____.

Then she told us to dip it in a pot of _____ 3 _____ and hang it on the

_____ 4 _____ to dry. Mine looked like a _____ 5 _____ that had stayed

in the pool too long. Next, each of us had to pick one _____ 6 _____ and glue a

sparkly _____ 7 _____ to the back. I couldn't help but wonder what our teacher

was up to! Then she said, "Class, I need you to each pass your _____ 8 _____

to the student on your right. When you get your new one, fold it into the shape of a

_____ 9 _____, take it home, and put it under your softest _____ 10 _____

as you sleep tonight." Now I understood! Our teacher wanted us to dream up an idea

for a new piece of _____ 11 _____ that we could hang next to our damp art from

today. I couldn't wait to see what my dream _____ 12 _____ looked like!

Twice as Nice

The hidden words your partner is finding are hidden objects, too. Can you find these 13 objects in the scene below?

eyeglasses

broom

teacup

crescent moon

bird

crown

comb

envelope

button

shark

spoon

nail

baseball

SANDWICHES

classic $6

BigTop $8

Teeny-Tiny $4

Twice as Nice

The hidden objects your partner is finding are hidden words, too. Can you find these 13 words in the letters below?

J	Z	U	S	B	D	F	Q	P	U	C	A	E	T	Y	K
Q	C	Y	F	H	Y	H	D	T	S	V	N	C	Q	D
W	B	B	D	I	C	H	V	L	R	E	C	R	O	W	N
M	U	H	K	S	Z	G	L	P	B	I	R	D	G	V	L
B	T	P	U	H	C	A	E	J	D	M	C	P	X	C	V
A	T	G	T	G	B	T	Y	E	N	V	E	L	O	P	E
S	O	B	P	E	N	I	E	B	J	K	M	R	D	Y	W
P	N	Q	S	L	A	Q	G	Z	R	T	I	D	X	X	J
O	O	A	J	T	I	H	L	V	A	O	N	J	Q	G	W
O	B	F	P	Y	L	F	A	O	B	R	O	M	X	C	I
N	D	S	O	C	R	E	S	C	E	N	T	M	O	O	N
I	S	J	F	D	I	E	S	U	Y	J	Y	Q	X	M	C
Q	M	O	H	Z	K	I	E	A	I	T	Z	Z	D	B	K
E	N	Q	I	H	D	E	S	T	P	Q	M	T	O	L	V

Word List

BASEBALL

BIRD

BROOM

BUTTON

COMB

CRESCENT MOON

CROWN

ENVELOPE

EYEGLASSES

FISH

NAIL

SPOON

TEACUP

109

Color Teamwork

 domino

 crown

 teacup

 coin

 plate

 slice of pizza

Make a basket with an assist! Work with your teammate to find all 12 objects in this scene. Then color it in together.

Art by Mike Moran

ice-cream bar

hockey stick

belt

umbrella

flying saucer

magnet

Mirror, Mirror

Each of these scenes contains the same 15 hidden objects, which are listed on the right. But the scenes are flip-flopped. Race your opponent to see who can find all 15 objects in his or her scene first!

banana   fish   mug   sailboat

bell   fishhook   paper clip   sock

canoe   heart   pencil   toothbrush

envelope   light bulb   ruler

Art by Kevin Rechin

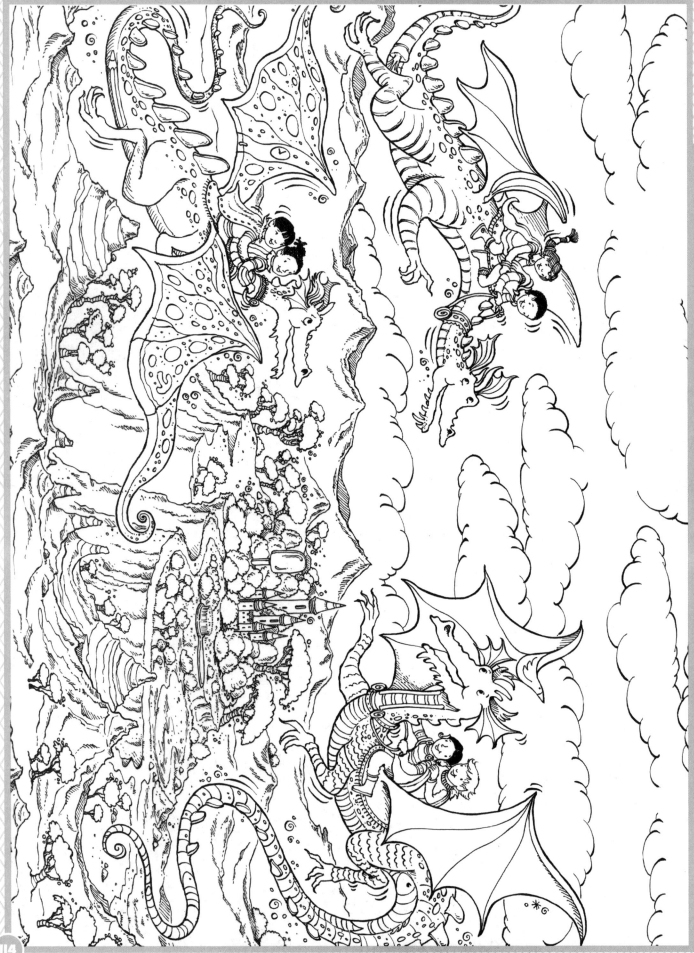

Guess and Seek

These are the 12 objects hidden in your friend's scene. Hold up this page and describe an object for your friend to find—without using its name. For example, you might describe a button as something you might find on your coat.

Take turns with your friend describing and finding objects. While your friend is finding objects, you can color in your scene.

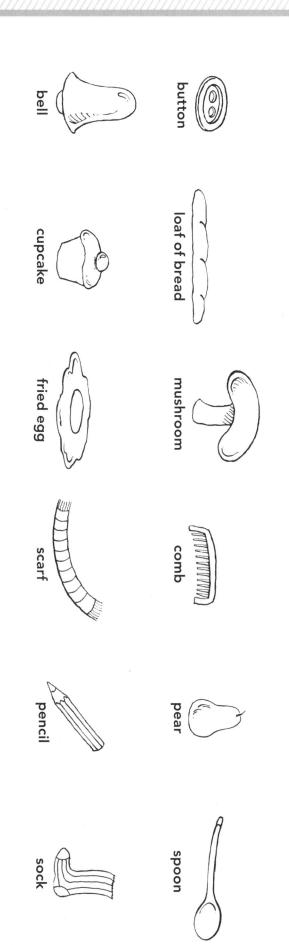

button

loaf of bread

mushroom

comb

pear

spoon

bell

cupcake

fried egg

scarf

pencil

sock

Dragon Riders

Guess and Seek

These are the 12 objects hidden in your friend's scene. Hold up this page and describe an object for your friend to find—without using its name. For example, you might describe a pencil as something you write with.

Take turns with your friend describing and finding objects. While your friend is finding objects, you can color in your scene.

banana

ice-cream bar

sock

worm

ladder

pencil

fish

wristwatch

bird

carrot

hairbrush

slice of pizza

Dragon Fires

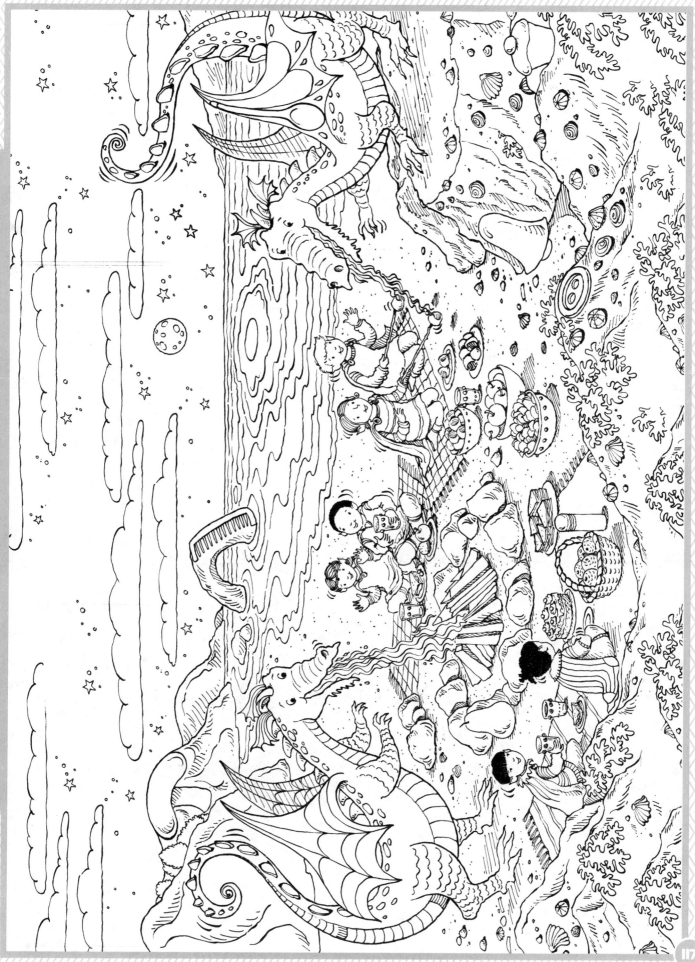

Words and Objects

There are 8 OBJECTS hidden on this page that match the 8 WORDS hidden on the next page. Work together to find them all.

There are 8 WORDS hidden on this page that match the 8 OBJECTS hidden on the previous page. Work together to find them all.

Art by Brian White

hide it!

Can you hide a pencil like the one below in a drawing? Hold up this page and draw your own Hidden Pictures® scene. Here are some ideas.

When you're finished, turn the book around so your friend can solve your Hidden Pictures® puzzle!

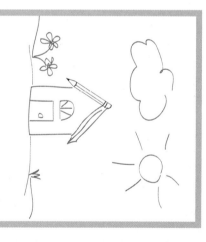

Art by Mike Moran

Hide It!

Can you hide a crown like the one below in a drawing? Hold up this page and draw your own Hidden Pictures® scene. Here are some ideas.

When you're finished, turn the book around so your friend can solve your Hidden Pictures® puzzle!

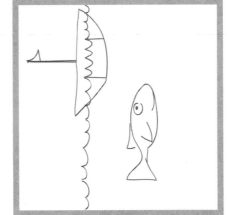

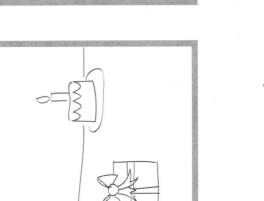

Seeing Double

Each object is hidden twice—once in each scene. Race your opponent to see who can find all 12 objects in his or her scene first!

bow
eyeglasses
mushroom
heart
pencil
umbrella
hockey stick
crown
crescent moon
musical notes
teacup
ladder

Art by Amy Schimler-Safford

Take Two

Each of these scenes contains 12 hidden objects, which are listed on the right. But each object is hidden only once. Which object is in which scene? Work with a friend to find all the objects.

adhesive bandage
banana
candle
carrot
comb
drinking straw
envelope
feather
heart
horseshoe
iron
needle
paintbrush
pencil
ruler
sailboat
saltshaker
slice of orange
slice of pie
slice of pizza
sock
spoon
teacup
toothbrush

Art by Neil Numberman

Our family went camping last weekend and, boy, was it a wacky _____!

First of all, my little sister packed so much! She brought her squishy
_____1_____, her favorite _____3_____ to play with, and even her
giant stuffed _____4_____. But that wasn't the craziest part. It all started when
we tried to set up the new _____5_____ to sleep in. My sister and I got most
of it up, but we couldn't find the last _____6_____ to finish it. We looked
everywhere. It wasn't under Dad's trusty camping _____7_____ or in mom's old
_____8_____. And it wasn't on top of the family _____9_____. Where
on earth could it be? Then we heard a crunching noise. "Oh, _____10_____!"
my sister yelled. Our pet _____11_____ was chewing on the last piece of
the tent! Drat! Good thing it was warm because we ended up sleeping under the
_____12_____, if you can believe it. But you know what? It wasn't so bad!

Silly Fill-In Story

Camp Out

Hold up this page. When your friend tells you the name of an object, write the name of that object in the first blank. Continue until all of the blanks are filled.

Silly Fill-In Story

Hold up this page and start searching for the 12 objects hidden in the picture.
When you find an object, tell your friend the name of that object.

Camp Out

 hockey stick

 ice-cream cone

glove

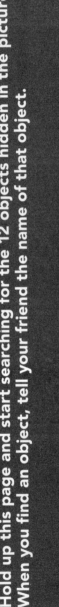 lollipop

 lamp

banana

artist's brush

 spoon

crayon

toothbrush

shoe

candle

Twice as Nice

The hidden objects your partner is finding are hidden words, too. Can you find these 14 words in the letters below?

Word List

- BUTTON
- CANDLE
- COAT HANGER
- CRESCENT
- MOON
- DOUGHNUT
- FEATHER
- FUNNEL
- GLOVE
- GOLF CLUB
- LADDER
- NEEDLE
- PENCIL
- PITCHFORK
- TOOTHBRUSH

```
N  T  N  C  R  E  S  C  E  N  T  M  O  O  N  Z
N  B  I  P  W  T  Z  P  B  N  E  E  D  L  E  W
D  K  U  Q  I  W  H  P  E  N  C  I  L  Q  K  F
O  K  H  T  V  T  B  L  F  G  L  O  V  E  L  Q
U  G  Q  K  T  C  L  J  S  U  E  O  V  X  M
G  O  Q  E  Y  O  H  O  B  F  N  L  P  O
H  L  F  C  H  O  N  S  F  O  N  U  N  Q  T  B
N  F  Z  W  W  T  L  V  T  O  T  E  R  E  G  H
U  C  O  A  T  H  A  N  G  E  R  E  Y  V  L  S
T  L  P  H  E  B  D  R  R  I  H  K  R  E  Y
C  U  O  B  R  D  U  R  T  B  D  C  H  U  L
Q  B  Q  O  C  U  E  O  A  B  D  U  L  Q
W  Q  T  U  P  S  R  E  O  Y  T  J  Q  E  A  Q
S  C  H  Y  P  H  F  Y  C  A  N  D  L  E  Y  Z
```

Twice as Nice

The hidden words your partner is finding are hidden objects, too. Can you find these 14 objects in the scene below?

 glove

candle

 button

pitchfork

doughnut

toothbrush

golf club

ladder

crescent moon

coat hanger

pencil

funnel

needle

feather

Color Teamwork

baseball bat

carrot

slice of pizza

sailboat

tack

comb

It's your turn to serve! Work with your teammate to find all 12 objects in this scene. Then color it in together.

Art by Jackie Stafford

 bell

 light bulb

 ax

teacup

eyeglasses

 lollipop

Mirror, Mirror

Each of these scenes contains the same 14 hidden objects, which are listed on the right. But the scenes are flip-flopped. Race your opponent to see who can find all 14 objects in his or her scene first!

banana

candy cane

cowboy hat

envelope

heart

leaf

open book

rolling pin

ruler

sailboat

slice of lemon

slice of pie

sock

toothbrush

Art by Brian White

Answers

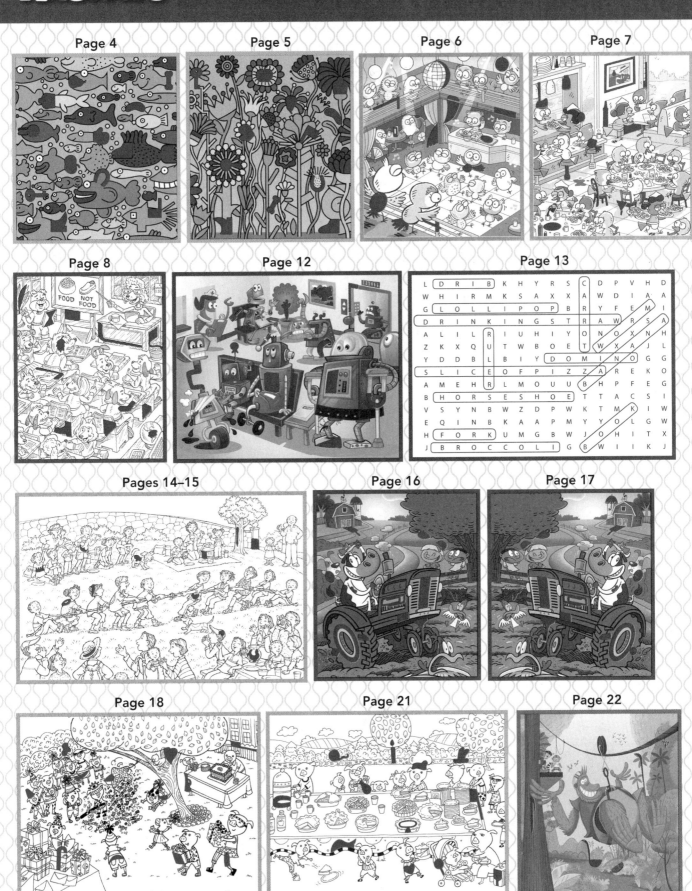

Answers

Page 23

Page 28

Page 29

Page 30

Page 31

Page 35

Page 36

N	W	I	I	A	F	H	F	L	I	U	T	E	K	K	C
R	F	Q	C	L	U	E	E	N	X	B	E	F	O	R	K
F	O	G	E	U	N	O	A	T	B	K	B	A	N	A	N	A
J	Z	Z	C	O	Z	E	G	T	N	S	U	P	V	P	S
Z	X	S	R	P	L	P	H	H	V	P	P	N	S	S	E
O	O	O	E	T	V	D	R	M	R	S	V	K	Z	J	H
N	W	B	A	M	H	E	R	M	C	M	C	P	T	S	O
Q	U	N	M	H	M	F	V	C	M	C	P	T	S	Y	E
C	Y	B	C	G	O	L	F	C	L	U	B	T	F	N	G
Y	L	S	O	N	A	P	T	R	T	U	G	W	O	A	J
R	T	U	N	J	S	P	O	O	N	J	B	L	A	R	R
B	A	S	E	B	A	L	L	D	D	L	G	F	S	B	G
B	F	S	C	I	S	S	O	R	S	O	T	S	X	P	I
E	Y	S	R	L	I	M	P	I	D	W	L	Q	Q	N	L

Page 37

Pages 38–39

Page 40

Page 41

Page 42

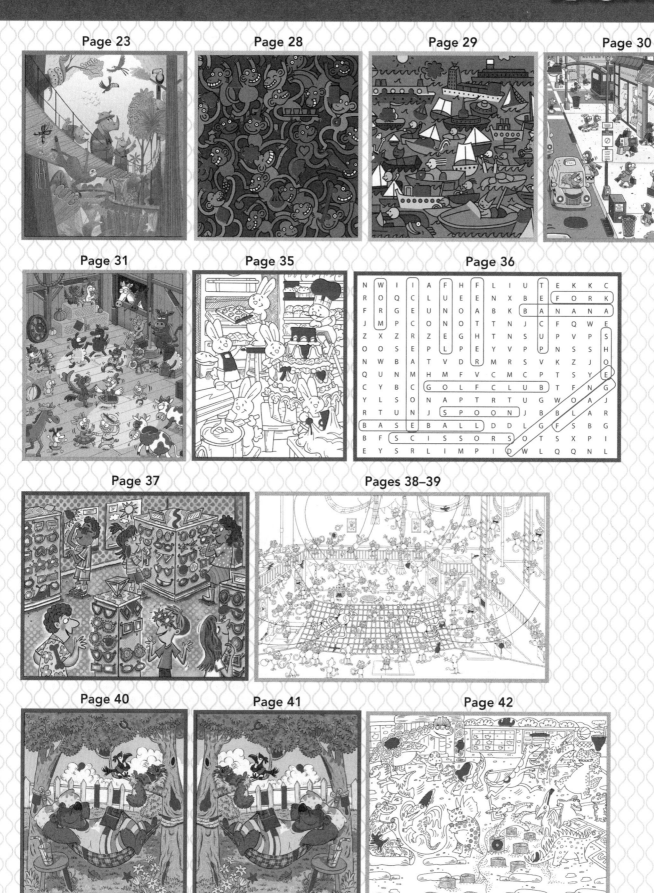

Answers

Page 45

Page 46

Page 47

Page 52

Page 53

Page 54

Page 55

Page 56

Page 60

Page 61

Pages 62–63

Page 64

Page 65

Answers

Page 66

Page 69

Page 70

Page 71

Page 76

Page 77

Page 78

Page 79

Page 83

Page 84
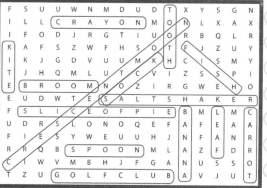

Page 85

Pages 86–87

Answers

Page 88

Page 89

Page 90

Page 93

Page 94

Page 95

Page 100

Page 101

Page 102

Page 103

Page 104

Page 108

Answers

Page 109

Pages 110–111

Page 112

Page 113

Page 114

Page 117

Page 118

Page 119

Page 124

Page 125

Page 126

Page 127

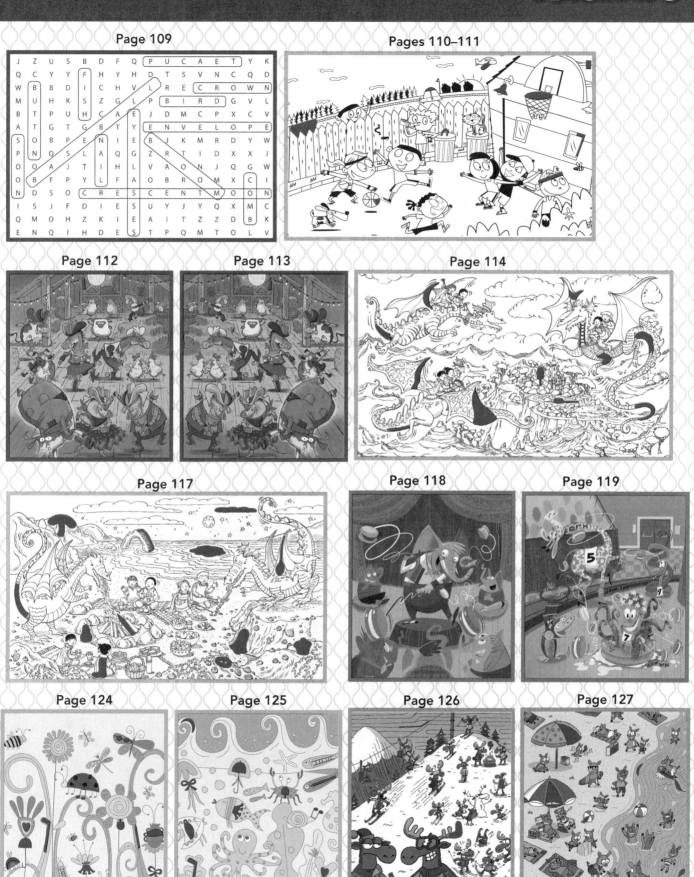

Answers

Page 131

Page 132

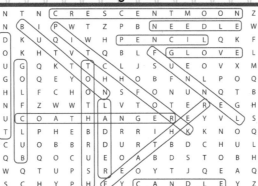

Page 133

Pages 134–135

Page 136

Page 137

Cover art by Neil Numberman

Copyright © 2018 by Highlights for Children
All rights reserved.

For information about permission to reproduce
selections from this book, please contact
permissions@highlights.com.

Published by Highlights for Children
P.O. Box 18201
Columbus, Ohio 43218-0201
Printed in the United States of America
ISBN: 978-1-62979-943-8

First edition
Visit our website at Highlights.com.
10 9 8 7 6 5 4 3 2 1